Contents

 4A Assessment

The Last Trick
page 2

 4B Assessment

The Final Battle
page 14

4A written by
Dee Reid

4A illustrated by
Dylan Gibson

4B written by
Diana Bentley

4B illustrated by
Peter Richardson

Series editor **Dee Reid**

Before reading The Last Trick

Characters

Cam

Ellie

Mr Wood

Tricky words

- thought
- assembly
- trouble
- unscrew
- detention
- sneaked
- change
- smiled

Read these words to the student. Help them with these words when they appear in the text.

Introduction

Cam and Ellie are friends. Ellie loves to think up cool tricks to play and she persuades Cam to join in, but Ellie's tricks end up with Cam getting into big trouble. He got into trouble when Ellie took a spider into assembly and when she made him unscrew the tops off the salt pots. Now Cam is in detention.

The Last Trick

Ellie thought of cool tricks to play.
She took a spider into assembly,
but it was Cam who got into trouble.

Ellie locked the loo doors, but it was Cam who got into trouble.

She got Cam to unscrew the tops off the salt pots and he got into trouble.

Now Cam was in detention. "You will be in detention up to 5pm," said Mr Wood.

But Mr Wood had to go out. Ellie sneaked in.

"I have thought of a cool trick to play," said Ellie.
"No way!" said Cam. "Your cool tricks got me in detention."

"No way!" said Cam. "**I** will keep a look-out and **you** can change the time on the clock."
"OK," said Ellie.

Ellie got on a chair to change the time on the clock.
"Cool or what?" said Ellie.

"Not cool," said Mr Wood, "I saw what you did."
"Oh!" said Ellie.

"Was it you who took the spider into assembly and who locked the loo doors?" asked Mr Wood.
"Yes," said Ellie.

"And did you make Cam unscrew the tops of the salt pots?" asked Mr Wood.
"Yes," said Ellie.

Quiz

Text comprehension

Literal comprehension
p4 Who had planned all the tricks?
p5 Who was in detention?
p7 What was Ellie's latest trick?
p9 How does Ellie's trick go wrong?
p11 What punishment does Mr Wood give Ellie?

Inferential comprehension
p8 Why do you think Cam insists that it is Ellie who changes the time on the clock?
p10 Why do you think Ellie owns up to all the other tricks?
p12 Do you think Ellie will play any more tricks?

Personal response
- Would you like a friend like Ellie?
- Would you play tricks like Ellie?

Spelling challenge

Study these words for one minute. Then write them from memory.

Phonically regular

think   that   came   time   gave

Irregular

what   could   were   coming   our

Ha! Ha! Ha!

How do you tell if a clock is hungry?

It comes back for seconds!

Before reading: The Final Battle

Characters

Twister

Scorcher

Chiller

Tremor

Agent Em

Agent Vee

Agent Que

Agent Zed

Tricky words

- suddenly
- crackled
- appeared
- shock-waves
- smashed
- ruler
- roared
- melted

Read these words to the student. Help them with these words when they appear in the text.

Introduction

The agents were in their Base when suddenly all the alarms went off and four evil faces appeared on their screen. It was Twister, Scorcher, Chiller and Tremor. They had all returned to kill the agents. The agents needed a plan, but before they could think of a plan, the super-villains arrived.

The Final Battle

The agents were in the Base when suddenly the alarms went off.

"We must stop them!" said Zed.
But before they could make a plan,
Tremor smashed into the Base.

"I will get you with my shock-waves,"
she roared. "Then I will be ruler of
the world."
But Tremor did not see Twister behind her.

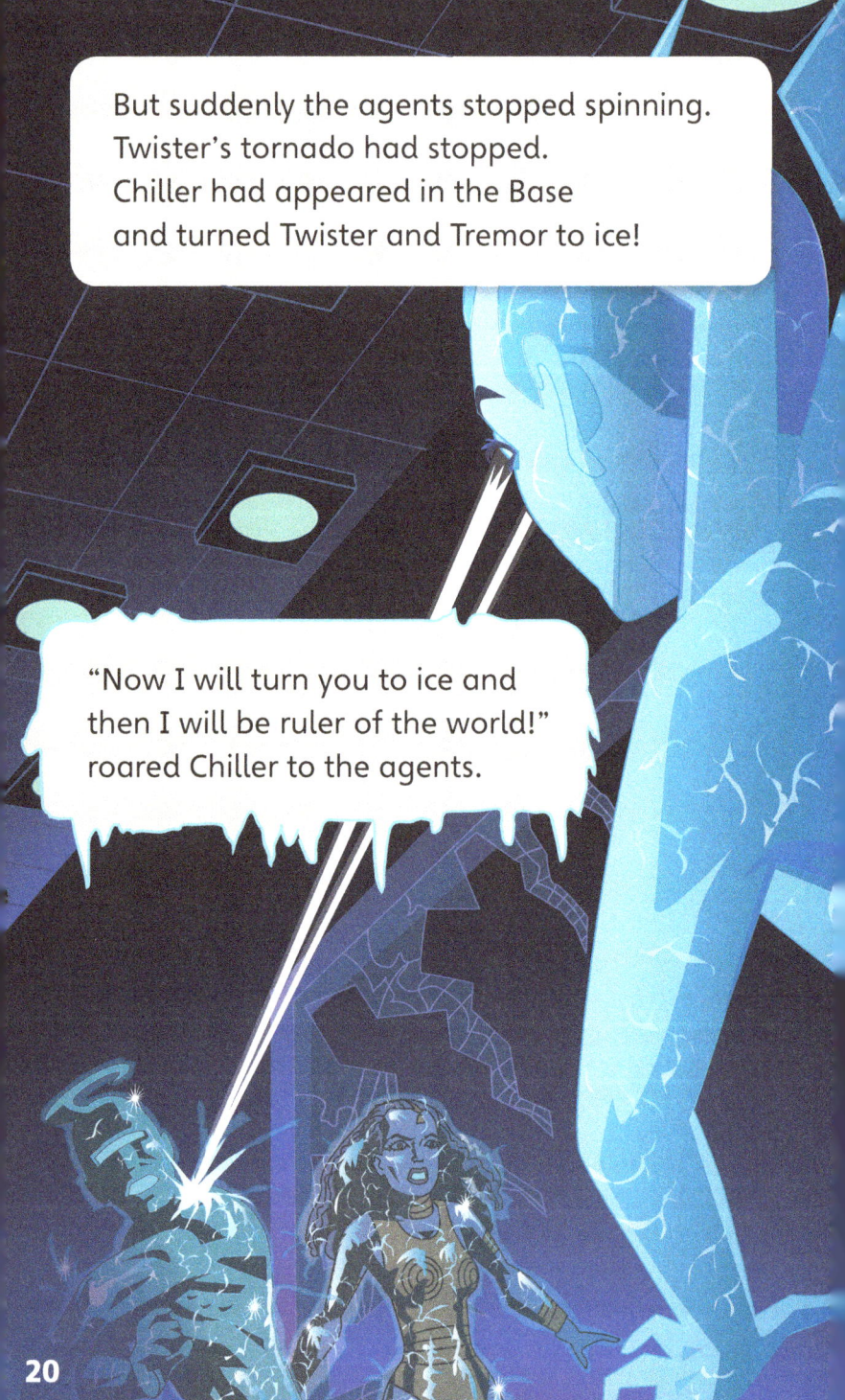

Chiller turned to look at Scorcher. She shot her ice-ray at Scorcher just as Scorcher shot fire at Chiller.

Quiz

Text comprehension

Literal comprehension
p15 How did the agents know the super-villains were on their way?
p19 How did Twister manage to get Tremor?
p20 What did Chiller threaten to do to the agents?
p23 What happened to Chiller when Scorcher shot fire at her?
p23 Why will the super-villains not be rulers of the world?

Inferential comprehension
p19 What was Twister's plan?
p20 Why did the agents stop spinning?
p23 Did the agents need a plan to stop the super-villains?

Personal response
- Do you think the super-villains were foolish?
- Do you think the agents were lucky?

Spelling challenge

Study these words for one minute. Then write them from memory.

Phonically regular

much   thing   when   next   wish

Irregular

would   having   any   always   first

Ha! Ha! Ha!

What is bright orange and sounds like a parrot?

A carrot!